The

Dysfunctional Family

Christmas Songbook

THE
Dysfunctional Family
CHRISTMAS
SONGBOOK

LYRICS BY
John Boswell AND **Lenore Skenazy**

ILLUSTRATIONS BY **Charles S. Pyle**

BROADWAY BOOKS
NEW YORK

A John Boswell Management Book

Library of Congress Cataloging-in-Publication Data
Boswell, John, 1945–
The dysfunctional family Christmas songbook/John Boswell and Lenore Skenazy—1st ed.
p. cm.
1. Humorous poetry, American. 2. Christmas—Poetry. 3. Family—Poetry. 4. Carols—Texts. I. Skenazy, Lenore. II. Title
PS3602.084D97 2004
811'.6—dc22   2004051810

First edition published 2004.

Book design by Nan Jernigan
Illustrated by Charles S. Pyle

ISBN 0-7679-1907-6
10 9 8 7 6 5 4 3

PRINTED IN THE UNITED STATES OF AMERICA

DEDICATION

John

To the extended Boswell family who taught me the
true meaning of dysfunction.

Lenore

To my dad, who always loved jokes, and my mom,
who will love me despite the ones in here.

ACKNOWLEDGMENTS

THANKS to Morry, Izzy, Hannah, Gigi, Joe (Lenore's
husband), Carol (John's wife), and Jessica Friedman for
their support and inspiration, and to David Fisher,
for playing matchmaker.

THANKS to our publisher, Charlie Conrad, editor Bill
Thomas, Michael Palgon, and Rex Bonomelli for
shepherding through a project that was far more
complex than it probably looks.

AND THANKS especially to Lauren Galit,
Christa Bourg, and Nan Jernigan whose
myriad contributions to this little tome are
way too numerous to list here.
We love you guys.

Table of Contents

COME MEET THE FAMILY

To the tune of *O Come All Ye Faithful*

Piano

O come meet the fam - ily, bad breeding tri-

umphant; O come meet the fam-i-ly dys- func- tion- al.

Come and be- hold them As they brag and fight and whine. For

it's a ce - le- bra-tion Of Christmas ag-gra- va - tion. And

if you're no re - la- tion, Just thank the Lord.

8

Come meet the drinkers,
Kleptos, kooks and stinkers.
Come meet the tattooed chick
And horny dog.
Don't miss the in-laws
Even though they'll make you puke.

For it's a celebration
Of Christmas aggravation
And if you're no relation,
Just thank the Lord.

Sing as you meet them,
Sing in exultation
Sing as you gather with
Your own nutty kin
Look at your family:
They could be a whole lot worse.

For it's a celebration
Of Christmas aggravation
And if you're no relation
Just thank the Lord.

9

GRANDPA'S DRUNK

To the tune of *Jingle Bells*

Piano

Ly-ing in the snow with his bour-bon at his side

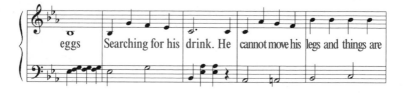

Grandpa's moving slow, Mouth hung open wide. Eyes like soft boiled

eggs Searching for his drink. He cannot move his legs and things are

get-ting bad I think. Oh Grandpa fell, Grandpa fell, Grandpa fell down

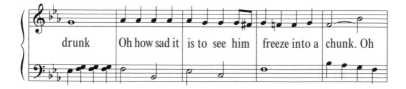

drunk Oh how sad it is to see him freeze into a chunk. Oh

Grandpa fell, Grandpa fell, Grandpa fell down drunk

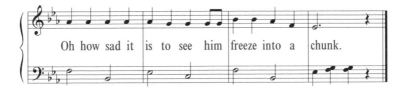

Oh how sad it is to see him freeze into a chunk.

Grandma limps around,
Lookin' mighty miffed
Spies an icy mound,
It's Grandpa or a drift

Runs out in her robe
To give him a fat lip.
When she tries to roll him home
She falls and breaks her hip

Oh Grandma fell, Grandma fell,
Grandma fell kerplunk
Oh how sad it is to see her freeze into a chunk.

Oh Grandpa fell, Grandpa fell,
Grandpa fell down drunk
Oh how sad to see both geezers freeze into a chunk.

Gloooooooria (not Glen)

To the tune of *Angels We Have Heard on High*

I like wear-ing | heels so high | when I lock the | bathroom door

Shoot some hormones | in my thigh | Sneak a peak at | Elle Decor.

Glo - oo — oo — oo oo— — oo oo — r - ia,

That will be my | new name. Glo - oo — oo — oo — ooo

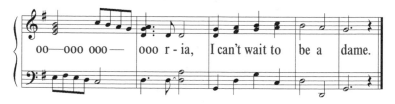

oo—ooo ooo — | ooo r - ia, | I can't wait to | be a | dame.

Years ago I felt the drive
Didn't know what I should do
Then I met a man named Clive
Who found a doc to make him Sue.
Gloooooooria, that will be my new name
Gloooooooria, I can't wait to be a dame.

Tell the fam on New Year's Day:
"Got someone that you should meet."
To the kitchen I'll sashay
Six foot four in nylon-ed feet.
Gloooooooria, that will be my new name
Gloooooooria, I can't wait to be a dame.

God Damn This Stupid Christmas Tree

To the tune of *God Rest Ye Merry Gentlemen*

Piano

God damn these stupid Christmas lights! Who wound them up this way? Re- member last year I was still un- tangling Christmas day? Did someone take this cord of lights and use it to cro- chet? Oh we tie things on branches that droop. Big friggin' whoop. We are tying things on branches that droop.

Let's not forget the popcorn string
That seasonal cliché.
Why is it no one mentions
Stringing one inch takes all day?
This trimming of the tree's as fun
As New Year's at AA.
We tie things on branches that droop
Big friggin'whoop
We are tying things on branches that droop.

And now get down the ornaments
We finally packed last May.
Those tacky, dime store ornaments
From back in Nixon's day.
There is just one that isn't broke
It's Barbie on a sleigh.
We'll tie her to branches that droop
Big friggin'whoop
We are tying things on branches that droop.

We Must Have a Perfect Christmas

HOMAGE TO MARTHA

To the tune of *We Wish You a Merry Christmas*

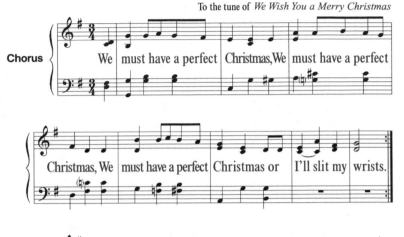

Chorus

We | must have a perfect | Christmas, We | must have a perfect

Christmas, We | must have a perfect | Christmas or | I'll slit my | wrists.

Piano

I | glue-gunned the | garlands so | they'd stay in | place. I

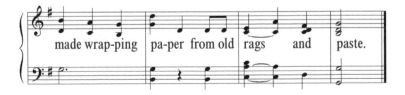

made wrap-ping | pa-per from old | rags and | paste.

I gathered cranberries
From out in the bog
I chopped down our elm tree
To make a Yule log.
Chorus

I raised my own duck
So I'd know what it ate
I killed it this morning
And now it's on your plate.
Chorus

So glad we can share
This holiday cheer
Touch my heirloom napkins
And I'll cut off your ear.
Chorus

If you spill a drop
On the cloth Martha made
Or pick up the wrong fork
I will have you filleted.
Chorus

I love what I do
With robins-egg blue
And if you don't think so
I'll glue-gun you too!
Chorus

HIT THE MALLS

THE KLEPTO SONG

To the tune of *Deck the Halls*

Piano

Hit the malls when they are hopping Fa la la la la la la la la

Get some gifts, but not by shopping Fa la la la la la la la la

Pick a pocket, rip some dude off Fa la la la la la la la la

Steal the red nose off of Rudolph Fa la la la la la la la la

Deck the guard who saw it happen
Fa la la la la la la la la
Leave him on the cold floor nappin'
Fa la la la la la la la la
Don me now a beard that tickles
Fa la la la la la la la la
Ring a bell and keep the nickels.
Fa la la la la la la la la.

Home I go with gifts like crazy
Fa la la la la la la la la
Shock my folks who think I'm lazy
Fa la la la la la la la la
Where'd it come from? I'm not tellin'
Fa la la la la la la la la
Merry Christmas, from your felon!
Fa la la la la la la la la.

O Holy Fight

Oh what a fight! The fists were really fly-ing; it was a fight that we'd heard more than once. "Lib-erals suck!" my uncle was im-plying, Till Dad ap-peared and said "Limbaugh's a dunce." A quick left hook, my father's drink went soaring and yonder broke our bust of F-D-R. "Fall on your knees!" crazed Uncle Doug was roaring. O

fight — so fine, O holy cow, O fight di-vine. O

fight — so fine, O holy cow, O fight di-vine.

Dad reeled around and rushed him, fists a-swinging
And did you know he was once Golden Gloves?
"Go burn a flag!" our Uncle Doug was singing
So much for ye brotherly love
The dog jumped in, and somehow pulled the rug out
My daddy tripped and fell into the tree
Crawled on his knees! And took a bite of Doug out
O fight so fine, O holy cow, O fight divine
O fight so fine, O holy cow, O fight divine.

Oh what a fight! The room was really rocking
Now they were back on the 2000 vote.
Doug slugged my dad, then grabbed a Christmas stocking
Which he wrapped right around Daddy's throat
My dad turned blue, his helpless limbs a-flailing
Till somehow he knocked Doug down to the floor
Brawled on their knees! The sirens came a-wailing
O fight so fine, O holy cow, O fight divine
O fight so fine, O holy cow, O fight divine.

Christina's World

To the tune of *Joy to the World*

Piano

Joy to the world, Chris-ti- na's here and I'm the

cut - est thing! Let ev - 'ry — one who's in— this

room turn a- round and watch me sing While I swi-vel like The

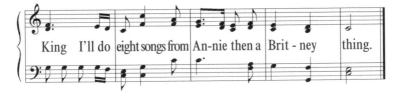

King I'll do eight songs from An-nie then a Brit - ney thing.

22

Wait, wait there's more! It's piano time
And you can hear me play!
I hope you like this piece
Its name is "Für Elise,"
Which I practice every day
When I get home from ballet
Now I'll put on my tutu and do my plié.

I do the splits, and cartwheels too
And last year I took tap!
I've got a treat for you
I'll tap to "Tea for Two"
Then I'll leap into the lap
Of my daddy while you clap
I'll be back with my puppets once I power nap.

A Jew's First Christmas

To the tune of *My Dreidel*

I am a lit-tle nervous This Christmas is my first. I like the tree and eggnog, but car-oll-ing's the worst. Oh Jesus, Jesus Je-sus He's there in ev-ery psalm. I'm singing songs of Jesus, just please don't tell my mom.

I knew what I was doing
When they asked me to come.
But where's the Manischewitz?
And what the hell's a sugarplum?

Oh Jesus, Jesus, Jesus
He's there in every psalm
I'm singing songs of Jesus
Just please don't tell my mom.

The family's very friendly
They say, "You're family, too."
But then they get the songbook
And sing to you-know-who.

Oh Jesus, Jesus, Jesus
He's there in every psalm
I'm singing songs of Jesus
Just please don't tell my mom.

The Mother-In-Law Song

To the tune of *Away in a Manger*

A- way in a— manger, is that where you

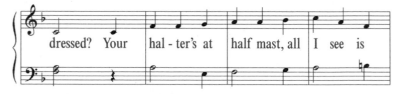

dressed? Your hal - ter's at half mast, all I see is

breast. You used your two "assets" to hog-tie my

boy. And now we -'re all fam - ily. I- mag-ine my joy.

I don't like to gossip, but look at Jim's date
Are twins in the picture or did she gain weight?
That mop on his forehead—no, I shouldn't talk
But throw a leash on it, I'm sure it would walk.

As sweet as our hostess may be, here's the truth:
Her breath smells like Listerine chasing vermouth
And too bad her youngest got dumped by her beau
I guess he got tired of dating a ho.

Thanks ever so much for inviting me here
Your side of the family's so different, my dear
The burping alone made this quite an affair
But off I must hurry to shampoo my hair.

So off I shall toddle, kiss, kiss, it's been fun
Too bad that the roast beef was so overdone
And as for the
company—best
wishes, rejoice.
I'll see you next
Christmas. I don't have
much choice.

Evil Brother Stevie

To the tune of *Good King Wenceslas*

Good King Wences-las looked out on my brother Ste-vie.

Never seen a boy so bad, not ev-en on TV.

Stevie took the can-dy canes from our ba-by nieces.

Rode his Big Wheel ov-er them, gave them back in pi - ec— es.

Stevie grabbed the Christmas wreath, wore it like a collar,
Wouldn't put it down unless Mom gave him a dollar.
"Wow, what's that?" our Stevie cried, pointing at the shutter.
While we turned, he fed the dog one whole stick of butter.

Stevie found the chocolate box, poked for something gooey,
Couldn't find one soft enough, so he hocked a loogie.
Spread it on a caramel cream, said, "This one looks yummy."
Sucked it up in front of us, rubbed his little tummy.

Good King Wenceslas was shocked, "That boy's off his axle.
He needs a good spanking and refills on his Paxil."
Stevie said, "Who cares? Your song isn't even edgy."
As the Good King turned to go, Steve gave him a wedgie.

DINNER SONG

To the tune of *Oh Little Town of Bethlehem*

Oh giant lump of shiny ham how still you sit to-night. Though you were made with love by Gram no-body took a bite. "I don't eat meat," said Cousin Pete and add-ed his wife Sue: "We all know that ham's full of fat and fat's not good for you."

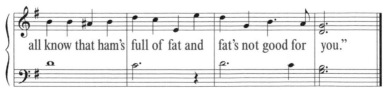

"Glazed ham is almost fiber-free," said Auntie with a nudge.
"Just take a bite, you'll see tonight: Your bowels will not budge."
"What's more," said Dad, a-looking sad, "on cooked food I don't sup.
Don't know 'bout you, but when I do I cannot get it up."

The little kids ate only fries, their folks on low-carbs chewed
Which left just me prepared to be the guest who eats real food.
But as I reached to take the ham my Gramps said Connie Chung
Once did a show and did I know that pigs eat their own dung?

It's been a year and still that dear old ham sits on the shelf
And dear old gram, just like that ham is looking grim herself.
She's not the same as when we came. She's lost her Christmas joy.
A vegan nut, she still cooks but next year the ham is soy.

THE BROTHER-IN-LAW SONG

To the tune of *Here We Come a Wassailing*

Piano

Here I come a- borrowing, I'm in a little bind.

Got a C-note you don't need? I knew you wouldn't mind.

Chorus

Oh, I need your car too. And I'll write an I-O-

U. And I pro - mise to get it back real soon, maybe by

June. Yes, I prom-ise you'll get it back real soon.

Merry Christmas, by the way,
You're looking very trim!
I've got a pal who needs a drill
Can I give yours to him?

Oh, I need your car, too
And I'll write an IOU
And I promise to get it back real soon
Maybe by June
Yes, I promise to get it back real soon.

Hey good buddy, I am back
And while we're standing here
I was kinda wond'ring if
You plan to drink that beer?

Oh, I need your car too
And I'll write an IOU
And I promise you'll get it back real soon
Maybe by June
Yes, I promise you'll get it back real soon.

WHOSE CHILD IS THIS?

To the tune of *What Child Is This?*

Whose child is this who pierced her breast, then dyed one pigtail and shaved the rest, Who bid goodbye to North Valley High to follow a punk band named Throb Quest? This, this sweet child of ours is hanging out in biker bars. If she'd just come get her mail, she would see her acceptance to Yale.

The day she left was a stormy one
When we'd only asked, "Is your homework done?"
She shrieked and cried
And she would have tried
To pierce some new part, but there was none.

This, this sweet child of ours is hanging out in biker bars
If she'd just come get her mail, she would see her acceptance to Yale.

She dropped a note when
She reached L.A.:
"I could not sell any blood today."
"P.S.," she wrote,
"On a lighter note—
Your very first grandchild
Is on the way."

This, this sweet child of ours
Is hanging out in biker bars
If she'd just come get her mail,
She would see her acceptance to Yale.

Silent Wife

To the tune of *Silent Night*

Silent wife, angry wife Say, "hello" Feel the knife. Every - thing I do makes her mad. Tells the kids, "Don't grow up like Dad." She won't leave me in peace! She won't leave me in peace.

Silent wife, glaring wife
She defines, "Marital strife."
When we dated, she cooed and she sighed
Now she's channeling Frankenstein's bride.
She won't leave me in peace!
She won't leave me in peace.

Silent wife, violent wife
Married her, ruined my life.
If you meet her, for goodness sake
Back out slowly and throw her a steak
She won't leave me in peace!
She won't leave me in peace.

THE FARTING SONG

To the tune of *Hark! the Herald Angels Sing*

Piano

Fart! Goes Cousin Harold's tooter. Loud enough to break a glass

He's just like a salad shooter When it comes to passing gas.

Joyfully, he makes his noise Loved by all the younger boys.

"Fart again!" his fans proclaim. "Let's see if you can light a flame!"

Hark! My cousin's mighty breeze Gloriously he cuts the cheese.

Fart! He's really in rare form
Listen to his golden ass
Softly now, with tone so warm
Followed by resplendent brass.
Rum pum pum, they keep on coming
Like that drummer boy, he's drumming.
Beans on toast is what he ate
No wonder he must percolate
Hark! My cousin's mighty breeze
Gloriously he cuts the cheese.

Fart! Oh no – the man's still tooting
Wonder when he's gonna stop?
Could we cite him for polluting?
Got more gas than soda pop.
Time to all the windows open
Will we breathe again? Here's hopin'!
"Jeez Louise!" the guests exclaim.
"Is there a Farting Hall of Fame?"
Hark! My cousin's mighty breeze
Gloriously he cuts the cheese.

O Hanging Time

To the tune of *Oh Christmas Tree*

Piano

O Christmas time, O Christmas time, The time all families hope for. I know I should be feeling good, So what'd I buy this rope for. I'm standing 'neath the chandelier and thinking I might dangle here. O Christmas time, pernicious time, No other time I mope more.

O Christmas time, O Christmas time
A time of deep foreboding.
I wear a smile
But in a while
I'll lace my punch with codeine.
And if I don't succeed tonight
I'll drown myself by morning's light
O Christmas time, sleep with fishes time,
The cops will find me bloating.

O Christmas time, O Christmas time
They've got the model trains out.
Should I go down
And play around
Or blow my bloody brains out?
I kinda hate to spoil the mood
And plus I smell my favorite food.
So Christmas time, I've changed my mind
I'll get the candy canes out.

Auld Dog Song

To the tune of *Auld Lang Syne*

Piano

Should old acquain -- tance be humped first as I

stand on legs so hind? Or should I hump this brand new guest? I

can't make up my mind. I guess I'll hump the old one first. Oh

yes, I'll hump him blind! And then I'll sneak up

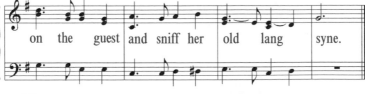

on the guest and sniff her old lang syne.

When I was just a tiny pup
I would play with ball and twine!
But now that I am all grown up
I poke where sun don't shine.
Oh yes, I poke my nose right in
So clammy, cold and wet!
That's simply my prerogative
As darling family pet.

Should unprepared guest find me rude
Because I'm so inclined
I'll back off, cute as Scooby Doo
Beloved by all mankind.
I'll cock my head and raise a paw,
Her brown eyes will meet mine
And when she comes to scratch my ears
I'll sniff her old lang syne.

Twelve Days of Cheapness

To the tune of *Twelve Days of Christmas*

Piano

On the first day of cheapness, my true love gave to me: A mug that he got at work free. On the second day of cheapness, my true love gave to me: Two bars of Dove and a mug that he got at work free. On the third day of cheapness, my true love gave to me: Three Bic pens, two bars of Dove and a mug that he got at work free. On the

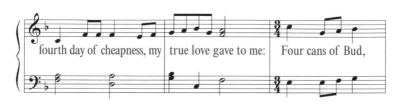

fourth day of cheapness, my true love gave to me: Four cans of Bud,

three Bic pens, two bars of Dove and a mug that he got at work free. On the

fifth day of cheapness, my true love gave to me: Five gumball rings!

four cans of Bud, three Bic pens, two bars of Dove and a

mug that he got at work free. On the free.

On the sixth day of cheapness, my true love gave to me
Six socks of Rayon,
Five gumball rings!
Four cans of Bud, three Bic pens, two bars of Dove
And a mug that he got at work, free.

On the seventh day of cheapness, my true love gave to me
Seven Swanson dinners, six socks of Rayon
Five gumball rings!
Four cans of Bud, three Bic pens, two bars of Dove
And a mug that he got at work, free.

On the eighth day of cheapness, my true love gave to me
Eight malted milk balls, seven Swanson dinners, six socks of Rayon
Five gumball rings!
Four cans of Bud, three Bic pens, two bars of Dove
And a mug that he got at work, free.

On the ninth day of cheapness, my true love gave to me
Nine ladies' razors, eight malted milk balls,
Seven Swanson dinners, six socks of Rayon
Five gumball rings!
Four cans of Bud, three Bic pens, two bars of Dove
And a mug that he got at work, free.

On the tenth day of cheapness, my true love gave to me
Ten quarts of Kool-Aid, nine ladies' razors, eight malted milk balls,
Seven Swanson dinners, six socks of Rayon
Five gumball rings!
Four cans of Bud, three Bic pens, two bars of Dove
And a mug that he got at work, free.

On the eleventh day of cheapness, my true love gave to me
Eleven plastic placemats, ten quarts of Kool-Aid, nine ladies'razors,
Eight malted milk balls, seven Swanson dinners, six socks of Rayon
Five gumball rings!
Four cans of Bud, three Bic pens, two bars of Dove
And a mug that he got at work, free.

On the twelfth day of cheapness, my true love gave to me
Twelve Dunkin'Donuts, eleven plastic placemats,
Ten quarts of Kool-Aid, nine ladies'razors, eight malted milk balls,
Seven Swanson dinners, six socks of Rayon
Five gumball rings!
Four cans of Bud, three Bic pens, two bars of Dove
And a mug that he got at work, free.